# Owl Eyes, Ears, and Fuzzy Rears?

## Fascinating Owl Facts

Written by
Jessica Lee Anderson

AO PRESS

Photos by
Bob Ferguson II

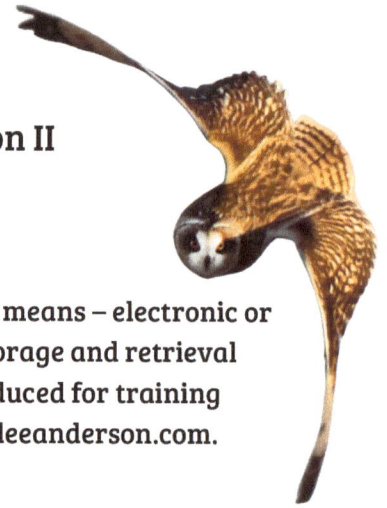

Paperback ISBN: 978-1-964078-61-8

To everyone who protects wildlife and wild spaces. - JLA

To my Step-daughter, Rebecca - You remind me that wisdom isn't just about knowing; it's about seeing with your heart. - BF

All photos taken by Bob Ferguson II apart from: P. 7: genphoto_art (Oriental Bay Owl); P. 8: (Northern White-faced Owl); P. 12: Nynke van Holten (Indian Scops Owl); P. 13: (Blakiston's Fish Owl) P. 24: bobloblaw (Burrowing Owl chicks and eggs); P. 32: Michael Anderson

Names of species (current iNaturalist common names) clockwise from top left, unless otherwise noted: Front cover: Central American Screech Owl; Title Page: Northern Saw-whet Owl; Copyright Page: Short-eared Owl; Dedication: Great Horned Owlets; P. 4: Short-eared Owl, Burrowing Owl, Red-tailed Hawk; P. 5: Eastern Screech Owl, Long-eared Owl, Screech Owl; P. 6: Snowy Owl flight combo, Northern Hawk-Owl flight combo; P. 7: Barred Owl, Oriental Bay Owl, Barn owl; P. 8: Eurasian Eagle-Owl, Boreal Owl, Northern White-faced Owl; P. 9: Eastern Screech Owl, Great Gray Owl, Great Horned Owls; P. 10: Northern Saw-whet Owl, Barred Owl, Barn Owl; P. 11: Great Horned Owlet, Barred Owl, Burrowing Owl; P. 12: Barn Owl, Indian Scops Owl, Eastern Screech Owl ; P. 13: Barred Owl, Blakiston's Fish Owl, Snowy Owl with Herring Gull; P. 14: Northern Saw-whet Owl, Spectacled Owl, Burrowing Owls; P. 15: Great Gray Owl, Barn Owl, Snowy Owl; P. 16: Eastern Screech Owls (top row), Great Horned Owl and Owlet; P. 17: Barn Owlets, McCall's Eastern Screech Owl, Burrowing Owl; P. 18: Ferruginous Pygmy Owl, Barred Owl, Mottled Owls; P. 19: Eastern Screeched Owl, Great Horned Owls, Boreal Owl; P. 20: Great Horned Owl, Snowy Owl, Burrowing Owl; P: 21: Burrowing Owl, Philippine Eagle-Owl, Eastern Screech Owl; P. 22: Ferruginous Pygmy Owl, Snowy Owl; P. 23: Great Horned Owl; P. 24: Burrowing Owl chicks and eggs, Barn Owl with egg, Great Horned Owl with Owlet; P. 25: Great Horned Owlets, Barn Owlets, Burrowing Owlet; P. 26: Great Gray Owl, Great Horned Owlet, Snowy Owl; P. 27: Great Horned Owl, Northern Hawk-Owl, Northern Saw-whet Owl; P. 28: Burrowing Owls, Mottled Owls, Long-eared Owls; P. 29: Central American Screech Owl, Barn Owl, Snowy Owl; P. 30: Elf Owl, Great Gray Owl, P. 31: Great Horned Owl, Snowy Owl, Short-eared Owl, P. 32: Northern Saw-whet Owl; Back cover: Barn Owl

**This Book Belongs to:**

_____

# Differences Between Owls and Hawks

Short-eared owl

Most owls are nocturnal (active at night), though a few owls like burrowing owls are diurnal like hawks (active during the day).

Owls and hawks are both birds of prey, meaning they are hunters with powerful talons and strong beaks. Owls have large eyes that face forward while hawks have eyes on the side of the head that see broader views without needing to move at all. Hawks have smaller heads in general, plus bodies built for speed. Owls fly silently and stealthily.

Red-tailed hawk

# Eyes

All birds have large eyes for their size, but owls have exceptionally enormous eyes! They don't have muscles that allow them to move their eyes the way you do. They always stare straight ahead, and to look at something, they will spin their head to get a better view.

Owls can spin their head around more than any other kind of animal—up to 270 degrees! (It is a myth that they can spin it all the way around.)

# Flight

Given specialized feathers and wing structures, owls fly silently through the air. Owls have a large wingspan compared to their body, which allows them to fly slowly and gently so they can quietly sneak up on their prey.

# Feathers

Owl feathers are made of keratin, the same protein as fingernails and reptile scales. They have a comb-like structure on the edge called flutings. This muffles noise as air rushes over the owl's wings. Owls can fly in light rain, though their feathers are not waterproof. Owls will often seek shelter in heavy rains and will fly again once their feathers dry.

Nocturnal owls have more developed feather flutings, helping them hunt quietly in the still of the night.

# Ears

Like you, owls have two ears, though their ears are hidden under feathers on either side of their head. Owls have asymmetrical ears—one ear points up while the other points down. This helps owls detect sounds above and below as well as side to side to find prey, even if completely hidden!

An owl's hearing is sensitive and superior to many other kinds of birds.

# Plumicorns?

"Horned owls" or "long-eared owls" among others may look like they have pointy external ears on the top of their head, but these are actually tufts of feathers called plumicorns. Scientists believe that plumicorns help with communication and camouflage.

Owls without tufts are called round-headed owls.

9

# Facial Disc

Owls have flat faces that are shaped like discs. They have many feathers on their face, especially surrounding their eyes. Specialized feathers direct sound waves to the owl's ears like a satellite dish.

Some owls like barn owls have heart-shaped faces. The facial disc is a hunting advantage!

# Beaks

All owls, even babies, have a sharp, curved beak that faces downwards. The hook at the end of the beak helps owls capture and eat prey items. An owl's beak continues to grow just like your fingernails, though hunting wears the beak down so it stays a healthy length.

Owls have two nostrils at the base of their beak. They rely more on their sense of hearing to hunt rather than their sense of smell.

# Natural Pest Control

Owls provide natural pest control services by preying upon rodents and insects that could potentially damage crops and possibly spread disease if left unchecked. Some people try to attract owls to barns and other places for pest control by making sure there are places to nest. They also avoid using insect and rat poisons that could harm the owls.

Certain owl species like this Indian scops owl eat mostly insects.

# Indicator Species

Owls, especially smaller species and the young, are vulnerable to other birds as well as mammals like coyotes. Owls are also vulnerable to changes in their environment, so scientists monitor populations to get a sense of the overall health of a habitat and the impacts of pollution. Owls are considered an indicator species as their presence indicates a healthy ecosystem.

If an owl population decreases, scientists use that as an early warning signal to help protect the ecosystem.

# Habitats

Owls live in a wide variety of habitats all over the world, apart from Antartica. They live in different kinds of forests as well as grasslands, tundra, and even desert environments.

# City and Country Owls

Many owl species have adapted to using human-made structures in both the country and the city.

# Nests

Owls do not build their own nests. They'll reuse old nests that other birds made, or they'll roost in tree hollows and other safe, secluded spots.

# Boxes and Burrows

Not all owls roost in trees. Some owls will find a place to rest in underground burrows. Others find shelter and raise their young in man-made wooden owl boxes.

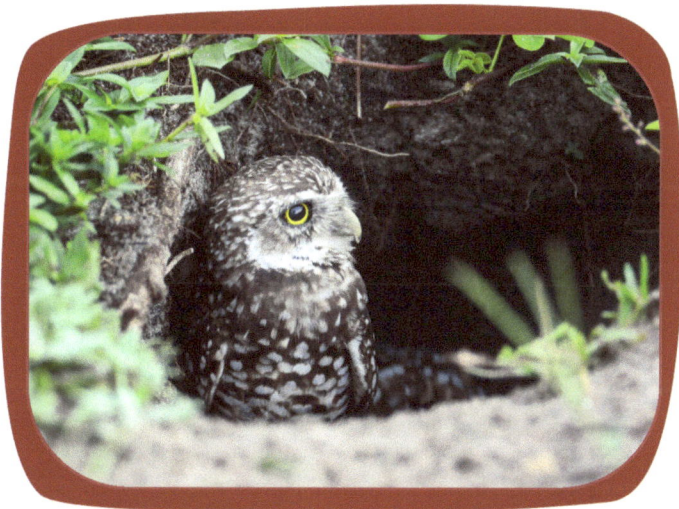

# Colors and Patterns

Feather colors and patterns vary by species, and many are mottled brown, grey, and white. As owls age, their coloration might change. Some owls are barred, or streaked, on their undersides and chest. Owl eye color varies from yellow to orange to black.

# Camouflage

Owl colors and patterns help owls camouflage, or blend into their habitat. Their feathers are often the same color and patterns as tree trunks and branches.

# Survival Strategies

Owls survive harsh conditions by conserving energy. Their dense feathers act like a blanket against the cold, and some species like snowy owls have feathers down to their talons! Certain species store food for later and get hydration from the food that they eat.

# Posture?

Owls use a variety of body postures as defense mechanisms if they sense a threat. Owls might stand tall and compress feathers against their body to avoid detection (concealment posture). Others might narrow their eyes to nothing more than thin slits. Certain owls may spread their wings to make themselves look larger.

# Whitewash?

Like reptiles, owls pass waste from an opening called a cloaca. (Some biologists even call owls avian reptiles as they are related to crocodilians and dinos!) An owl's waste (pee and poop) is semi-liquid and looks like white chalk when it dries, hence the name whitewash. Whitewash can be a sign of an owl's recent presence.

# Owl Pellets?

Owls often swallow prey whole. The hard, undigested bits of food (such as bones, teeth, and fur) get compacted by a stomach organ called a gizzard. Owls will then regurgitate (throw up) the pellets.

# Eggs

Owls reproduce by laying eggs. Female owls will often line the nest with shredded pellets before laying a clutch of eggs. Depending on the species, clutch sizes range from two eggs to a dozen or more. Usually, the female sits on the eggs to incubate them while the male brings her food. Owl eggs hatch at different times, typically in about a month on average.

# Owlets?

Owl chicks are known as owlets. Downy, fluffy feathers provide warmth. The down will be replaced by feathers as the owlets grow. Owlets depend on their parents to provide food until they mature and fledge the nest to hunt on their own.

# Fluffy Rears?

Owlets have fluffy, downy rears. Adult owls have tail feathers called retrices they use to steer and brake. Contour feathers cover an owl's body and provide shape and insulation. They fill in the area at the base of an owl's tail.

# Molting

Owls regularly shed and replace all of their feathers in a process called molting. Healthy feathers are important for flying and survival! During a molt, owls may look scraggly. This is an itchy, vulnerable time for owls! Molting takes energy, plus losing feathers can impair an owl's ability to fly.

# Social Groups

While some owl species may live alone, others like long-eared owls roost together in the winter for warmth (communal roosting). Certain owls like burrowing owls live in groups, and they sometimes coexist with other species like prairie dogs. Young owls stay with their family while they mature.

# Communication

Owls communicate by making sounds like hoots, hisses, whistles, barks, and screeches. The sounds and meanings are unique to specific species. Some owls will snap their beaks or clap their wings together if threatened.

# From Small to Large

The elf owl is the world's lightest and smallest species of owl, about the length of an average pair of sunglasses. The great gray owl is one of the largest owl species in terms of length and wingspan. Their wingspan is as wide as the height of some adult humans!

# Otherworldly Owls

There are about 250 different kinds of owl species in the world. Colombia has the most owl species.

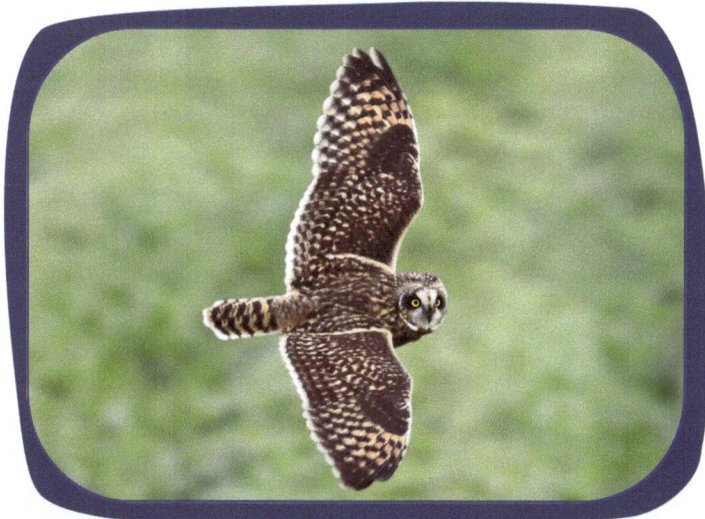

Scientists are continuing to learn more about owls. Given their unique looks and characteristics, owls are often associated with mystery and wisdom, and they're popular in art and literature.

Jessica Lee Anderson is an award-winning author of over 100 books for young readers. Jessica loves spending time in nature and exploring the outdoors with her husband, Michael, and their daughter, Ava! A great horned owl often visits her backyard in Austin, Texas. You can learn more about Jessica by visiting www.jessicaleeanderson.com.

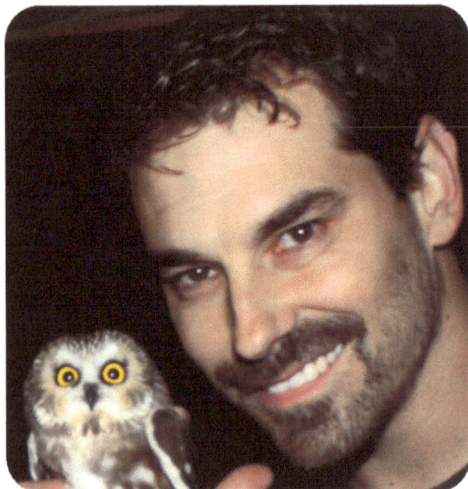

Bob is a naturalist with a compulsion to be outdoors. Wildlife conservation through entertainment, education, fundraising, and fieldwork is his mission and purpose in life. His organization, Fascinature, has donated six figures to saving land in the world's most biodiverse spaces. He even has a frog named after him! You can find him on Instagram @bob_ferguson_fascinature or sign up for his newsletter at fascinature.live.

## Check out these other books!

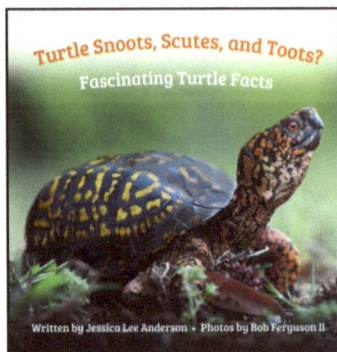

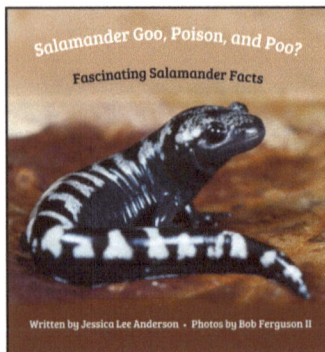

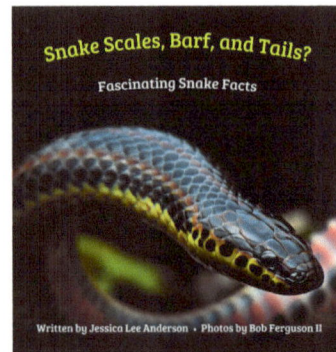

Turtle Snoots, Scutes, and Toots?
Fascinating Turtle Facts
Written by Jessica Lee Anderson • Photos by Bob Ferguson II

Salamander Goo, Poison, and Poo?
Fascinating Salamander Facts
Written by Jessica Lee Anderson • Photos by Bob Ferguson II

Snake Scales, Barf, and Tails?
Fascinating Snake Facts
Written by Jessica Lee Anderson • Photos by Bob Ferguson II

www.ingramcontent.com/pod-product-compliance
Lightning Source LLC
Chambersburg PA
CBHW061145030426
42335CB00002B/114